My First Animal Library

Porcupines

by Mari Schuh

Bullfrog
Books

Ideas for Parents and Teachers

Bullfrog Books let children practice reading informational text at the earliest reading levels. Repetition, familiar words, and photo labels support early readers.

Before Reading
- Discuss the cover photo. What does it tell them?
- Look at the picture glossary together. Read and discuss the words.

Read the Book
- "Walk" through the book and look at the photos. Let the child ask questions. Point out the photo labels.
- Read the book to the child, or have him or her read independently.

After Reading
- Prompt the child to think more. Ask: Have you ever seen a porcupine? Where were you? What was the animal doing?

Bullfrog Books are published by Jump!
5357 Penn Avenue South
Minneapolis, MN 55419
www.jumplibrary.com

Library of Congress Cataloging-in-Publication Data

Schuh, Mari C., 1975– author.
 Porcupines / by Mari Schuh.
   pages cm. — (My first animal library)
 Audience: Ages 5–8.
 Audience: K to grade 3.
 Summary: "Vibrant photographs and carefully leveled text introduce emergent readers to the porcupine as it looks for food and defends itself against a predator. Includes picture glossary and index."—Provided by publisher.
 Includes bibliographical references and index.
 ISBN 978-1-62031-290-2 (hardcover: alk. paper) — ISBN 978-1-62496-350-6 (ebook)
 1. Porcupines—Juvenile literature. I. Title.
 II. Series: Bullfrog books. My first animal library.
 QL737.R652S38 2016
 599.35'97—dc23

                                                    2015030639

Editor: Jenny Fretland VanVoorst
Series Designer: Ellen Huber
Book Designer: Michelle Sonnek
Photo Researcher: Michelle Sonnek

Photo Credits: All photos by Shutterstock except: age fotostock, 13; Alamy, 18–19; Corbis, 3, 4, 20–21; CritterZone, 16–17; Dreamstime, cover; Getty, 5; Science Source, 24; SuperStock, 6–7.

Printed in the United States of America at Corporate Graphics in North Mankato, Minnesota.

Table of Contents

Full of Quills

What is that?

A porcupine!

A porcupine is a rodent.
It has long front teeth.

It has long hair.

quills

It has quills, too.
The quills are sharp.
They keep it safe.

The porcupine
looks for food.

It climbs a tree.

It gnaws on bark.

Yum!

bark

Oh no! A puma!

Go away!

The porcupine grunts.

It shakes.

Thump! Thump!

It stomps its feet.

Its quills stand up.
Now it looks bigger.

Oh no!

The puma got too close.

Ouch!

Its paws are full of quills.

The puma runs away.

The porcupine is tired.
It is time to rest.

Parts of a Porcupine

nose
A good sense of smell helps porcupines find food to eat.

guard hairs
Long guard hairs help keep porcupines dry.

claws
Porcupines have long, sharp claws.

tail
Some porcupines have a short tail. Others have a long tail.

Picture Glossary

bark
The hard outer covering of a tree.

quills
Sharp, stiff hairs on a porcupine's back, sides, and tail.

gnaw
To keep biting or chewing on something.

rodent
A mammal with long front teeth used for gnawing.

Index

To Learn More

Learning more is as easy as 1, 2, 3.

1) Go to www.factsurfer.com

2) Enter "porcupines" into the search box.

3) Click the "Surf" button to see a list of websites.

With factsurfer.com, finding more information is just a click away.